... to the Jew first

RAMON BENNETT

SHEKINAH

JERUSALEM

All *italics* within the text are Scripture quotations.Those in ***bold italics*** are used for emphasis.

Written permission must be secured from the author to use or reproduce, ***by any means***, any part of this book, except for brief quotations in reviews or articles.

ISBN 978-1-943423-23-1

Published in the United States by Shekinah Books LLC

Distributed in Israel by: Ramon Bennett,
P. O. Box 37111, Jerusalem 91370.
eMail: armofsalvation@mac.com.

SHEKINAH

Shekinah Books LLC
A division of *Arm of Salvation Ministries,* Jerusalem.

Further copies of this book can be obtained by logging onto:
http://www.shekinahbooks.com.

A bruised reed he will not break, and a dimly burning wick he will not extinguish

(Isaiah 42:3).

Two peoples

Apparently, in the mind of God Almighty (Hebrew, אל שדי) there are only two peoples in the world: Jews and non-Jews. Of those two peoples He chose the Israelites, the descendants of His friend Abraham (*the Hebrew* — Genesis 14:13), through the line of his son Isaac, to be a special nation and he made a covenant with them and said:—

> *Now therefore, if you obey Me fully and keep My covenant, you shall be My treasured possession among all the peoples* (Exodus 19:5).

Being chosen by God Almighty as His own special treasure is truly a great honor, but this causes many Jews to act wretchedly toward non-Jews and spitefully use them. Some Jews, mostly educated rabbis, hold to the belief that the worldwide non-Jew majority of 7.7 billion (2020) was created only to serve the worldwide minority Jew population of 14.7 million (2020). Such is the general belief among Jews who believe that because they are the chosen race they are in every way superior to non-Jews. Some Jews see the two types of peoples as being connected to the biblical injunction to differentiate between what is clean and pure, and what is unclean and impure. Thus for them the two types of peoples become the two types of food animals, the clean, which are pure and permitted to be eaten by Jews, and the unclean, which is forbidden food for Jews and which is not simply not clean, but is positively unclean, polluted, impure, an abomination.

An ultra-Orthodox (Haredi) rabbi explained his understanding of clean and unclean by saying to a non-Jewish man: "We Jews are the clean animals, we are righteous inside and out. You Gentiles are the unclean animals, related to the pig that wallows in its own filth." When the rabbi began to utter his hostile diatribe his wife asked him to stop, but, being supremely confident of his own 'righteousness' he was not deterred from humiliating the non-Jew. Such a discourse would not be termed antisemitic because it is a non-Jew that was being insulted. Antisemitism is when non-Jews disparage Jews, but apparently there is no clear-cut term for Jews that disparage non-Jews. Many

Jews can be disgustingly offensive in their comments toward non-Jews without fear of being tarred and feathered for their insulting remarks.

For all their wholly self-perceived righteousness, Haredi (ultra-Orthodox) Jews are habitually charged with corruption, theft and sex crimes by law enforcement officers in Israel and in the diaspora. (Many Haredi Jews refer to themselves as Hassidic, which is an Haredi subset, a spiritual movement begun in Poland in the 18th century and whose main religious and philosophical idea is the worship of God through joy.) Haredi is a biblical term that means "one who trembles before God" and comes from the book of the prophet Isaiah:—

But this is the one to whom I will look,
to the humble and contrite in spirit, who
trembles at my word (Isaiah 66:2b).

The Hebrew word for "tremble" is חרד – *hared,* thus we have the adopted name for tens of thousands of pious Jews. Unfortunately, many so-called Haredi Jews are hypocrites; far from being pious and far from being *"humble and contrite in spirit"* many are often labeled as sexual abusers of both males and females and are reported as such in the media. A one-off evil sexual deed is usually insufficient to make a headline in Israel news, but when an Israeli ultra-Orthodox man was arrested in August 2019 and indicted for sexually abusing forty-five underage girls, that did make the news.

Also making world headlines, and had been making them for months, is Malka Leifer, who has, at this time of writing, had sixty-eight court dates in Israel over a period of six years fighting extradition to Australia to face seventy-four charges of child sex abuse. Leifer was the principal of a Haredi Adass Israel School for girls in Melbourne, Australia, and the school administration purchased plane tickets for her to flee to Israel prior to the Australian police issuing an arrest warrant. At this time of writing the Jerusalem District Court in Israel has accepted the prosecution's argument that Leifer has been feigning mental illness to avoid extradition and has given permission for Leifer's extradition proceedings to go ahead in the Supreme Court.

Israel police are also charging former Israeli Health Minister Ya'akov Litzman, an ultra-Orthodox politician who heads Agudat Yisrael (part of the United Torah Judaism alliance) in the Knesset (Parliament), with obstruction of justice by making false reports concerning Leifer's health in attempts to prevent her extradition and facing trial. Leifer has ties to Litzman's Gur sect of Haredim, the largest and most powerful ultra-Orthodox sect in Israel.

Another prominent Israeli ultra-Orthodox rabbi, Eliezer Berland—who has a cult-like following and is affiliated with the Breslov Haredi movement—is once again in the news after being indicted for defrauding his sick and elderly followers out of millions of dollars. These charges are in addition to a parallel case in which he was arrested after hundreds of complaints for selling prayers and "wonder drugs"—which turned out to be across-the-counter medications and candy—to desperate members of his congregation, promising families that those with disabilities would be able to walk, and for promising families with convicted felons that they would be freed from prison. Berland was formerly the subject of a years-long international manhunt before being arrested and sentenced to eighteen months in prison in 2016 on two counts of indecent acts and one case of assault after being accused of sexually assaulting followers.

In June 2020, Berland was again making headlines when the President and two other "highly respected" rabbinical judges of the renowned Bnei Brak rabbinical court determined—after eighteen months of proceedings in a special court it had established—that there is "irrefutable testimony," which leaves no doubt that Berland had committed "severe" sexual crimes by "repeatedly" touching married and single women under their clothes. The President and judges called upon the public to distance themselves from Berland.

Also, in August 2020, Matti Ben-David, an ultra-Orthodox director of a Jerusalem-based advertising agency, was sentenced to 17 years in prison for sexual assault against six ultra-Orthodox women he employed. In addition to the prison sentence, Ben-David was ordered to pay $140,000) in compensation to the complainants. The Jerusalem District Court convicted Ben-David on charges of rape, sodomy and indecent acts on six of his employees, against their will.

In addition there are also a few corrupt ultra-Orthodox members of Israel's Knesset (Parliament) awaiting official police indictments for corruption at this time of writing. One of whom is Aryeh Deri, the Minister of the Interior, Minister of the Development of the Negev and Galilee and a member of Israel's Security Cabinet. Deri is the leader of the Shas ultra-Orthodox political party who in 1999 was convicted of bribery, fraud and breach of trust and sentenced to three years in prison. Deri reentered political life after several years, was reappointed as leader of Shas and reelected to the Knesset. In November 2018 Israel Police and the Israel Tax Authority recommended the State Attorney's Office again indict Deri, this time on charges of fraud, breach of trust, tax evasion, obstruction of justice, money laundering, and making a false declaration.

It is not like there is no corruption among non-ultra-Orthodox members of the government (in 2018 Israel was placed at number 34 on a scale of 180 countries, 1 being the least corrupt), but it is the ultra-Orthodox who tirelessly claim to be "righteous," which in many cases is about as far south of the truth as it is possible to get.

In May 2017 even a former Ashkenazi Chief Rabbi of Israel, Yona Metzger, was sentenced to prison for forty-one months after pleading guilty to fraud, theft, conspiracy, breach of trust, money laundering, tax offenses and accepting millions in bribes.

Ultra-Orthodox Jews in Israel comprise only around eleven percent of the population. There are many God-fearing, law-abiding Jews in that number, but there are very many who are criminals in nature, who have not yet been apprehended by law enforcement officers; they bring dishonor to their fellow ultra-Orthodox but even more sadly, they dishonor God Almighty before whom they claim to tremble:—

You who boast in the law dishonor God by breaking the law. For, as it is written, "The name of God is blasphemed among the Gentiles because of you"
                                   (Romans 2:23–24).

Those who have been mentioned above as criminals are but the tip of the iceberg, and the rabbi who told the non-Jew that he was "related to the pig that wallows in its own filth" and that Jews are "righteous inside and out" also stole from the man by taking $500.00 for a computer part ticketed at $150.00.

jews and gentiles

Non-Jews are universally termed 'Gentiles', written with a lowercase first letter when written by a Jew or referenced in an English-Language newspaper or magazine owned or published by Jews. Rules of grammar necessitate an uppercase first letter when referencing a definite object or group, and Gentiles, written with an uppercase first letter, would be correct. However, very many Jews perceive Gentiles to be inferior to Jews, therefore Gentiles are referenced as 'gentile' or 'gentiles,' which highlights perceived Jewish superiority. Jew is always referenced with an uppercase first letter.

Perhaps it is time to level the playing field and reference jew, jews and all things jewish with lowercase letters like jews are accustomed to doing with 'gentile,' but it would most certainly bring a tsunami of hysterical screams of "Antisemitism!" from English-speaking jewish protestors. From a jewish standpoint, the use of a lowercase 'j' could point to a hatred of jews and all things jewish and would likely be seen as blatant antisemitism.

Settling that grammatical question would be about as simple as arriving at a peaceful settlement to the insuperable Israel-Palestinian conflict.

Hebrew

Non-Hebrew speakers should understand that there is no letter "J" in the Hebrew alphabet. In English Bible translations all names beginning with "J" are merely English renditions of Hebrew names beginning with י (Yod), which transliterates as a Y, thus Jacob in Hebrew (reading from right to left) is יעקב, which transliterates as Ya'akov.

Jeshua

Jesus is the Greek form of Joshua, which is the same as Jeshua. The name Jeshua is mentioned twenty-seven times in the books of Ezra and Nehemiah: Jeshua was the High Priest after Israel's return from the Babylonian Captivity: —

> Then **Jeshua the son of Jozadak** and his brethren the priests, and Zerubbabel the son of Shealtiel and his brethren, arose

*and built the altar of the God of Israel,
to offer burnt offerings on it, as it is
written in the Law of Moses the man of
God* (Ezra 3:2).

Joshua

The name Joshua is mentioned eleven times
in the books of Haggai and Zechariah. Joshua
and Jeshua are one and the same person. He
was the High Priest following Israel's return
from her seventy-year captivity in Babylon:—

*So the Lord stirred up the spirit of
Zerubbabel the son of Shealtiel,
governor of Judah, and the spirit of
Joshua the son of Jehozadak, the high
priest, and the spirit of all the remnant
of the people; and they came and worked
on the house of the Lord of hosts, their
God* (Haggai 1:14).

Jeshua in Hebrew is a shortened form of
Joshua, while Joshua in Hebrew is itself a
shortened form of Jehoshua. All three Hebrew
names share the one basic meaning despite
the plethora of meanings put forward over the
ages by well-intentioned people. However
the name chosen by the LORD and given to
Joseph, the husband of Miriam (Mary), was

Jeshua (Hebrew, ישוע), not Joshua (Hebrew, יהושע). Jeshua has come down to us in the name's Greek form of Jesus. Obviously, God Almighty had a reason for naming His Son Jeshua (ישוע). Just as Jeshua was the High Priest after the Captivity in Babylon, so Yeshua (Jesus/ישוע) is the High Priest *"according to the order of Melchizedek"* (Hebrews 6:20) after the captivity to sin. Whereas all were once banished from God's presence due to mankind's fallen nature, those who believe in Yeshua (Jesus) can now enter the Holy of Holies and approach God Almighty's throne with confidence (Hebrews 10:19).

Salvation

By far the most common explanation of the meaning of Jesus (Hebrew, ישוע) has been "Salvation." Perhaps this is because it has been read into the message given to Joseph about Miriam (Mary), which was:—

> *And she will bring forth a Son, and you shall call His name Jesus (ישוע), for He will **save** His people from their sins*
> (Matthew 1:21).

Or possibly it was assumed from Simeon's discourse:—

*LORD, now You are letting Your servant depart in peace, according to Your word; for my eyes have seen Your **salvation** which You have prepared before the face of all peoples, a light to bring revelation to the Gentiles, and the glory of Your people Israel* (Luke 2:29-32).

No matter how it may have come about, this writer does not feel Salvation is the correct meaning of the name Jesus, and this for the following reasons:—

The word "salvation" in Hebrew is (ישועה) (Yeshuah), not ישוע (Yeshua). Following are three examples of the word ישועה (Yeshuah) used in the Old Testament:—

*The LORD has made known His **salvation** (ישועה); His righteousness He has revealed in the sight of the nations* (Psalm 98:2).

*Indeed He says, "It is too small a thing that You should be My Servant To raise up the tribes of Jacob, And to restore the preserved ones of Israel; I will also give You as a light to the Gentiles, that You should be My **salvation** (ישועה) to the ends of the earth"* (Isaiah 49:6).

*Thus says the LORD: "Keep justice, and do righteousness, For My **salvation** (ישועה) is about to come, And My righteousness to be revealed"*

(Isaiah 56:1).

The LORD is speaking above about making His salvation ישועה (Yeshuah) known through His Son ישוע (Yeshua/Jeshua), giving him as a light to the the nations (for that is what the word Gentiles usually means), that there will be no salvation available to man apart from through His Son, and that He will come again soon ("soon" being in God's context, not ours). But none of this means to say that ישוע (Yeshua/Jeshua) the name of the Creator's only begotten Son means "Salvation."

ישוע (*Yeshua/Jeshua*)

The name of God Almighty's Son is ישוע (Yeshua/Jeshua), and for the real meaning of the name this writer believes the reader will find it in an ancient Hebrew ceremony that was in vogue for thousands of years.

Turning to Reuben Alcalay's eminent 7,000 page Hebrew/English Dictionary that includes "cultures for all periods," we find just one entry that includes the word ישוע

(Yeshua/Jeshua), and the entry in Hebrew is (reading from right to left): ישוע הבן (Yeshua HaBen) while the English meaning set forth there is: "ceremony of **redemption** of the firstborn son."

God Almighty says *"Israel is my firstborn son"* (Exodus 4:22) therefore this writer believes the name "Yeshua" (ישוע / Jesus) must surely mean "**Redemption**" rather than "Salvation." And when he hung on the cross at Calvary ישוע (Yeshua/Jeshua/ Jesus) took upon himself the sin of the world and **redeemed** mankind. From the moment he uttered: *It is finished!* (John 19:30) — the last word in the redemption of mankind — until the resurrection of the dead on the last day (John 6:39, 40, 44, 54; 11:24 & 12:46), every human being who will accept the LORD's redemption and truly believes in his or her heart that ישוע (Yeshua/Jeshua/Jesus) is God's only begotten Son will be sealed with the Holy Spirit of God Almighty and shall have everlasting life.

The body will return to dust, but the spirit will live on eternally, where that will be depends upon our personal choices: Accepting the redemption ישוע (Yeshua/Jeshua/Jesus) wrought for us on the cross means we shall spend eternity in the presence of our Creator in a new and righteous world (2Peter 3:13; Revelation 21:1). Those who reject God's redemption will live and linger on, eternally banished from His glorious presence and power (2Thessalonians 1:9), suffering the destruction of all enjoyment, dignity, honor, holiness and happiness.

Sin in the Garden

Due to their rebellion and sin against God Almighty, Adam and Eve were driven from *"Eden, the Garden of God"* and banished from His presence. Also, the Israelites were twice driven from the Promised Land—*the LORD's land* (Leviticus 25:23; Hosea 9:3)—because of their sins and they, too, were banished from His presence. Although the Jews were given the land of Canaan thousands of years ago and subsequently called it the land of Israel, the Jews have only had—according to an historian—full possession of all the land for little more than two hundred years; sin always brought an end to their occupation one way or another. We all inherited Adam's sinful nature and sin has brought disease and death to mankind, effectively banishing man from God's presence. Believing oneself to be "righteous inside and out" does not make it so. Believing God Almighty, as Abraham did, is the only way to be righteous in God's eyes:—

> *And he (Abram) believed the Lord, and He counted it to him as righteousness*
>   (Genesis 15:6)

Another person whom God Almighty counted as righteous was Phinehas, the grandson of Aaron the high priest. In the twenty-fifth chapter of Numbers we read that while Israel was staying at Shittim, the Israelites began having sexual relations with the women of Moab and a devastating plague from the LORD broke out:—

> *One of the Israelites brought a Midianite woman into his family, in the sight of Moses and in the sight of the whole congregation of the Israelites. When Phinehas son of Eleazar, son of Aaron the priest, saw it, he got up and left the congregation. Taking a spear in his hand, he went after the Israelite man into the tent, and pierced the two of them,*

the Israelite and the woman, through the belly. So the plague was stopped among the people of Israel

(Numbers 25:1–8).

God Almighty took notice of this act and said:—

Phinehas son of Eleazar, son of Aaron the priest, has turned back my wrath from the Israelites by manifesting such zeal among them on my behalf that in my jealousy I did not consume the Israelites

(Numbers 25:11).

And thus we read:—

Phinehas stood up and intervened, and the plague was stopped. And that was reckoned to him as righteousness from generation to generation forever

(Psalms 106:30-31).

Righteousness is reckoned to us by God Almighty when we *believe Him* and and act on His behalf and according to His precepts. Religious ultra-Orthodox Jews who lie, cheat, evade taxation, sexually molest women, girls or males; who steal, accept bribes, commit fraud, launder money, *et al*, are further from being righteous than the ninety-three million mile distance between Earth and Sun.

There is a huge difference in the way many Haredi Jews view themselves: "righteous inside and out," and the way God Almighty views His chosen people:—

> *The fool says in his heart, "There is no God." They are corrupt, they do abominable deeds; there is none who does good.*
>
> *The Lord looks down from heaven on the children of man, to see if there are any who understand, who seek after God.*
>
> *They have all turned aside; together they have become corrupt; there is none who does good, not even one*
>
> (Psalms 14:1–3).

In John chapter 3 we find the following:—

> *There was a man of the Pharisees named Nicodemus, a ruler of the Jews. This man came to Jesus by night and said to him, "Rabbi, we know that you are a teacher come from God; for no one can do these signs that you do unless God is with him." Jesus answered and said to him, "Most assuredly, I say to you,*

unless one is born again, he cannot see the kingdom of God." Nicodemus said to him, "How can a man be born when he is old? Can he enter a second time into his mother's womb and be born?" Jesus answered, "Most assuredly, I say to you, unless one is born of water and the Spirit, he cannot enter the kingdom of God. That which is born of the flesh is flesh, and that which is born of the Spirit is spirit. Do not marvel that I said to you, 'You must be born again.' The wind blows where it wishes, and you hear the sound of it, but cannot tell where it comes from and where it goes. So is everyone who is born of the Spirit"
(John 3:1-8).

Yeshua – ישוע (Jeshua/Jesus) put a great deal of emphasis upon being born again, born of the Spirit of God. We are all born naturally of the flesh, with Adam's sinful nature. In order to live in the presence of the LORD in the Kingdom of God we must be born again, from above, with God's own nature. Just as we came through water in a natural birth (the birth begins when our mother's sack of water in which we are floating, breaks), so we must be baptized by immersion and then clothed and filled with the Spirit of the Living God. After we are born again, and only then, we are restored back to God and become his sons and daughters. This is the **redemption** that ישוע (Yeshua/Jeshua/Jesus) won for us on the cross. ישוע (Yeshua/Jeshua/Jesus) was God incarnate and he took responsibility for sin and took it all upon himself, redeeming us from the consequences of sin. The reason that salvation is so easy is because it cost God Almighty so much.

The story of the Jews and God Almighty, their Maker, is a love story which ultimately has a happy-ever-after ending, but there is a long way to go before the ideal is realized.

Before the advent of Christianity there had been centuries of enmity between Jews and non-Jews, but the crucifixion of Yeshua (Jesus) opened Pandora's box and let antisemitism hold sway over millions of illiterate Gentiles who were accepting Christianity. Many ignorant Gentile converts swallowed the hatred and lies spewed out against the Jews by the clergy of the developing Church for having killed Christ, because they were ignorant of both the facts and the truth. The Jews themselves have tried to shift the blame for the crucifixion onto the Romans who had—at the instigation of the Jews, together with their loud vocal encouragement to crucify Yeshua (Jesus)—driven the spikes through his hands and feet and nailed him onto a Roman cross. The Jews did not hammer the nails through his hands and feet, because they were not permitted to do so under Roman rule, but they would have if they could have done so because the Jewish religious leaders wanted ישוע (Jesus) dead. The Jews have, unsuccessfully, spent two thousand years trying to convince the world that they had nothing to do with the crucifixion of Yeshua (Jesus) and have attempted to put the entire blame upon the Romans. But the Roman Governor dismissed that and passed the guilt back to the Jews (see pages 68-69). After two thousand years of denying Jewish involvement, only Jews believe Jews had nothing to do with the crucifixion of Yeshua (Jesus).

However, it was neither Jew nor Gentile that was responsible for the death of Yeshua (Jesus). Sin was responsible for his death. It was sin—the reader's sin and this writer's sin—that crucified him. God purposely sent His Son to be the atonement for the sin of he world. Yeshua (ישוע/Jesus) came intentionally, and for no other purpose, than to die for the sin of the world on a Roman cross.

Multitudes of Gentiles who became Christian were totally Bible ignorant. They knew nothing about the prophesied coming of a Jewish Messiah who would be put to death as a sacrifice for the sin of the world. Most Jews were fully Bible literate and were expecting their Messiah to come, but closed their eyes and ears to the prophecies of his coming, which is fully in accord with God Almighty's word:—

> *And He said, "Go and say to this people: 'Keep listening, but do not comprehend; keep looking, but do not understand. Make the mind of this people dull, and stop their ears, and shut their eyes, so that they may not look with their eyes, and listen with their ears, and comprehend with their minds, and turn and be healed.'"* (Isaiah 6:9–10).

When the Messiah finally came the Jews largely rejected him because he was very often highly critical of the religious leaders and he did not fit their perception of a nationalistic, conquering leader. The Jews should have known from the Scriptures that the Messiah would not be a warrior King, but rather a man of peace: —

> *For to us a child is born, a son is given to us; and the government will be upon his shoulders. And he will be called Wonderful Counselor, Mighty God, Everlasting Father, Prince of Peace*
>
> (Isaiah 9:6).

> *And you, O Bethlehem of Ephrath, least among the clans of Judah, from you one shall come forth, to rule Israel for Me— one whose origin is from old, from ancient times; and this one shall be peace* (Micah 5:5).

Many Jews quickly accepted and embraced their Messiah. Scholars believe there were about sixty-eight thousand believing Jews at the time of the destruction of the Second Temple. Those Jewish Christians believed what Yeshua (Jesus) had said about the end time and the coming destruction of the temple and did as he instructed, they fled Israel, the largest number fleeing to Pella, Jordan. Few ever returned.

Yeshua (Jesus) the Stone of stumbling

The very early Church was completely Jewish and those Jewish Christians suffered dreadful persecution at the hands of their Jewish brethren because, as the Prophet Isaiah said, Yeshua (Jesus) would be:—

> *A stone men strike against: a rock men stumble over for the two houses of Israel, and a trap and a snare for those who dwell in Jerusalem* (Isaiah 8:14).

However, despite the violent opposition the Jewish Christians encountered, they held to their conviction and deep faith in the *"gospel of God"* and took the message of the cross and the atonement through Yeshua (Jesus) throughout Israel and across borders. They began changing the world.

Wherever Christians took the message of the cross they were violently opposed by Jews living in the exile (diaspora) because Yeshua (Jesus) and the cross was:—

> *a stone of stumbling and a rock of offense — The stone that the builders rejected has become the chief cornerstone*
> (Psalms 118:22).

According to historical records much of the Jewish opposition and violence came about through jealousy, because Gentiles were far more receptive to the message of the atoning work of Yeshua (Jesus) on the cross than Jews were, which did not sit well with all those opposed to the message, it was like pouring oil on the flames. It is recorded by a New Testament writer that:—

> *by hindering us from speaking to the Gentiles so that they may be saved they have constantly been filling up the measure of their sins; but God's wrath has overtaken them*

(1Thessalonians 2:16).

The coming of the Messiah is a continuous theme throughout the Hebrew Bible, from Genesis to Malachi. And the prophecy given by God Almighty to Abraham that all nations would be blessed through him because of his faith and righteousness is also clearly portrayed in the Hebrew Bible. It is also clear that the Gentiles of the world would seek after God's Messiah and bow down to him. Yet some 2,000 years following the advent of Messiah the Jewish people, by and large, refuse to heed the message of the Hebrew

Bible and will go to great lengths to prevent Jews from hearing and accepting the message of the cross. Rabbis have always controlled Jewish religious thought and some parts of the Hebrew Bible, like Isaiah chapter 53, are forbidden for Jews to read in the synagogues because it shows the suffering of Yeshua (Jesus) the Jewish Messiah. Rabbis have gone to great lengths to prevent Jews from recognizing and accepting their promised Messiah. Yeshua (Jesus) made few friends among the religious hierarchy of the day by saying (as an example) to the multitudes that followed him:—

> *For I say to you, that unless your righteousness exceeds that of the scribes and Pharisees, you will by no means enter the kingdom of heaven*
>
> (Matthew 5:20).

Traditional Jewish dates of remembrance have also been shuffled around because observing them on their original days would lead to a showing of Yeshua (Jesus) to be the Messiah. So, religious leaders colluded together to move days and dates around in order to prevent other Jews from putting two and two together and coming to faith in their Messiah. Pointing out religious hypocrisy made Yeshua (Jesus) no friends among the pecking order of the religious hierarchy. Speaking of the *"Kingdom of God,"* Yeshua (Jesus) lit into the lawyers: —

Woe to you lawyers! For you have taken away the key of knowledge. You did not enter in yourselves, and those who were entering in you hindered (Luke 11:52).

The above quotation is from the gospel according to Luke, the third of the four gospel narratives contained in the New Testament. Testament is an old English word meaning, "covenant," or "agreement between two parties." It was derived from the Latin *testamentum*. This term was used to translate the Greek and Hebrew words for covenant; *berit* in Hebrew and *diatheke* in Greek. Thus the Old and New Covenants became the Old and New Testaments. This is the ancient meaning of the term.

However, the two sections of Scripture are not "testaments" in the modern sense of the word, as in: "last will and testament," rather, the term speaks of an agreement, a covenant or a contract. It is unfortunate that the word "testament" is still used in English to describe the Old and New Covenants that God made with His people.

Many ultra-religious Jews will opine that the New Covenant or New Testament does not exist, but with hundreds of millions of Christians believing its teachings, to say that it does not exist is singularly obtuse. Clearly, the different gospel narratives in the New Testament, which were largely written from memory and directed at different groups, contain some conflicts, but there are also many conflicts in the Hebrew Bible—there are none so blind as those who do not wish to see.

All but two of the twenty-seven books that make up the Greek Canonical New Testament were written by Jews who believed the Lord, the other two books Luke and the Acts of the Apostles, were written by a Gentile believer of God. At least a few of the New Covenant (Testament) books were originally written in Hebrew, but none have remained extant, although there are several references to them in the writings of the early Church fathers.

The New Covenant, which many millions

of Jews stubbornly refuse to recognize, came about because Jews did not act in accordance with the Old Covenant, which was God's plan A. The Jews did not keep the Old Covenant so God put plan B into action, but not before He gave advance warning:—

> *The days are surely coming, says the* LORD, *when **I will make a new covenant** with the house of Israel and the house of Judah. **It will not be like the covenant that I made with their fathers** when I took them by the hand to bring them out of the land of Egypt—a covenant that they broke, though I was their husband, says the* LORD. *But this is the covenant that I will make with the house of Israel after those days, says the* LORD: ***I will put my law within them, and I will write it on their hearts;** and I will be their God, and they shall be my people*
> (Jeremiah 31:31–33).

It seems rather obvious that if the LORD says He is going to make a new covenant, then the old covenant—the old agreement; the Mosaic or Sinaitic covenant; the Old Testament—will be superseded by a new agreement; a New Covenant, which is the New Testament.

A covenant is a formal agreement, a pact, a promise. It is a contract to which both parties must adhere otherwise it is null and void. The Israelites failed miserably in adhering to the original covenant that God made with them when He took them by the hand and brought them up from Egypt, so He promised them a new Spiritual covenant, one which would be in them and one which He would write on their hearts once it was personally accepted. But relatively few Jews have accepted the New Covenant, largely due to pressure from rabbinical leaders and the obfuscation of God Almighty's signposts pointing to the Messiah. Yeshua (Jesus). Yeshua (Jesus) laid his life down, becoming:—

> *a servant of the circumcised on behalf of the truth of God, in order that he might confirm the promises made to the patriarchs* (Romans 15:8).

Abram (Abraham) believed the LORD

It was the continuous breaking of the Mosaic or Sinaitic Covenant with its six hundred and nineteen commandments contained in the first five books of the Hebrew Bible, known as the Torah—the Law—which necessitated the making of a new covenant, one that could be kept. Had the Jews kept the Mosaic or Sinaitic there would have been no need for a new covenant and they would have had the same righteousness accounted to them as was accounted to Abraham for having believed the Lord four hundred and thirty years before the Mosaic covenant came into effect: —

And he believed the Lord; and the Lord reckoned it to him as righteousness
(Genesis 15:6).

Very few Israelites emulated Abraham and believed the Lord or kept His covenant. It was a sad day when the psalmist was moved by the Holy Spirit to write: —

They have all gone astray, they are all alike perverse; there is no one who does good, no, not one (Psalm 14:3).

And God rebuked the general mass for its proud spirit, but approved those who were righteous through faith: —

Look at the proud!
  Their spirit is not right in them, but the righteous live by their faith
(Habakkuk 2:4).

It is a simple matter of Law versus faith. A majority of Jews today *believe in* the LORD, but it is a very small minority that actually **believe the** LORD, else they would believe what He says about the promised Messiah and not hide His words away from His covenant people. As James, the brother of Yeshua (Jesus), writes to those under the law (but who never kept it): —

> *You believe that there is one God. You do well. Even the demons believe—and tremble!* (James 2:19).

Under plan A, the Old Covenant—the Mosaic Law—people must keep all the ordinances and commands from God in order to be deemed righteous in His eyes. To break a single command was to break the entire Law. Keeping all the commands and ordinances proved impossible and was meant, over time, to be seen as being impossible, until plan B came into force. Plan B was meant to show how futile a person's endeavors were to keep the Law; the law was a guardian, as the writer of the book to the Galatians explains: —

> *So then, the law was our schoolteacher until Messiah came, in order that we*

*might be justified by faith. But now that
faith has come, we are no longer subject
to a schoolteacher* (Galatians 3:24).

The early Church was entirely Jewish for some eight years before the gospel was preached to the Gentiles. The early Church was vibrant, full of the Spirit of God, and the lives of people and nations were changed. Then the rot set in. After the Bar Kochba revolt the Romans banned Jews from Jerusalem and the headship of the Church was lost to the Jews. The Bishop of Rome took over and assumed the headship of the Church and within a few decades it became political and polluted with greed and lust for wealth and its leaders hungry for power. The Roman Church soon literally ruled nations and kings and teachings of Yeshua (Jesus) and the apostles were only adhered to by a minority that loved God more than they loved the Church. Of the hundreds of millions today who profess to be Christian, only a small percentage actually are, the vast majority are "Christians" in name only.

The Church lost its way and the biggest enemy of the Church today is the Church itself. This writer thanks the LORD for the relative few that still cling to the teachings of Yeshua (Jesus) and the apostles. But because the Church has lost its way it does not let the Jews off the hook. The Jewish religious leaders still obstruct the spreading of the gospel, still obstruct the people of "the book" from believing what is written in "the book"—"the book" being the Hebrew Bible.

Just as the Church itself is the biggest problem that faces the Church today, so the Jews themselves are the biggest problem facing the Jewish people today. The Haredi (ultra-Orthodox) Jews comprise about eleven percent of Israel's population and virtually worship their rabbis, venerating them above all else, even the word of God. They are unable to think for themselves, they are akin to Catholics who also do not think for themselves but must ask their priests for guidance on matters clearly stated and explained in the Bible.

Comparative Populations

Israel is the worldwide homeland for Jews, but the influence of the small percentage of ultra-Orthodox Haredi Jews has the country listed among the nations of the world with the most restrictive laws and policies regarding religious freedom. According to a study by the *Pew Research Center,* released in July 2019, its rankings put Israel only one place behind Iran, and in some categories Israel is even keeping company with the likes of Saudi Arabia.

In the *Pew* study Israel was placed at number 13, one place after Iran in the category of restrictions on religious freedom worldwide. Tens of thousands of extremist ultra-Orthodox (Haredi) Jews are the Jewish equivalent of the Muslim Taliban. They are willfully stubborn and spiritually obtuse. If ultra-Orthodox Jews could kill Christians, destroy their churches and shrines and get away with it like the Taliban and the Islamic State do, they would. Over the years numbers of churches and convents in Israel have been desecrated, vandalized and firebombed, and an occasional attempt at murder has been recorded. Hatred festers inside many hearts of ultra-Orthodox Jews and, just like the Taliban and the Islamic State, the Haredi sects fight among themselves for group supremacy.

The Jewish people have a very long history among the peoples of the world, equal to that of China and India; however, that being said, the comparisons end.

In mid-2020 China had a population of 1.438 billion people, and India's mid-2020 population was 1.377 billion. In mid-2020 Israel's Jewish population was 6.7 million.

According to Israel's Central Bureau of Statistics, there was a total of 14.7 million Jews worldwide at the end of 2018, just short of the 14.8 million that were alive in 1925. Seventy-five years after the end of World War II the Jewish people had not yet recovered the number it had before the outbreak of the war.

About 3,500 years ago (scholars differ on the exact timeline) the Israelites—the descendants of Abraham through Isaac—left Egypt after more than four hundred years—of which many were spent as slaves of the Egyptians—and journeyed toward Canaan, which later became known as the Land of Israel. The Hebrew Bible informs us that in total, but excluding the tribe of Levi:—

from twenty years old and upward, ***everyone able to go to war in Israel***—*their whole number was six hundred three thousand five hundred fifty. The Levites, however, were not numbered by*

their ancestral tribe along with them
(Numbers 1:45–47).

This amount was not the number that came out from Egypt, these were only the Israelite warriors, troops fit for waging war. As to be expected, some scholars dispute the numbers, but the Hebrew Bible definitively states that the number of those able *"to bear arms"* was six hundred three thousand five hundred fifty.

As in most populations, females would make up approximately fifty to fifty-one percent of the population, so we can now safely double the number given for those males able to bear arms, which gives us one million two hundred seven thousand one hundred. However, we are not finished. We must add to that number all the males and females below the twenty-year conscription age, and also of those who were either too old or too weak to bear arms. There must surely have been about the same number as those who bore arms, therefore we add another six hundred three thousand five hundred fifty, which gives us a rough tally of one million, eight hundred ten thousand, six hundred fifty (1,810,650) people coming out of Egypt.

Critics will likely say there is no evidence that such a large number would have come out from Egypt because, unlike modern-day picnickers who despoil every eye-pleasing spot they find, the Israelites did not leave heaps of plastic bags, plastic plates, plastic cups and eating utensils, bottles and soda cans. Cooking pots and other utensils brought from Egypt would have got taken into Canaan, and at the end of their journey God Almighty told the Israelites: —

> *I have led you forty years in the wilderness. Your clothes have not worn out on you, and your sandals have not worn out on your feet*
> (Deuteronomy 29:5).

Cooking utensils, clothing and footwear lasted throughout the journey so, apart from the faithless generation from the age of twenty years and upwards, which subsequently died out over a period of forty years and was buried in the vast area of the wilderness, there would have been little evidence of such a horde having passed through.

Of the one million, eight hundred ten thousand, six hundred fifty (1,810,650) Israelites who came out of Egypt, an entire generation from the age of twenty years upwards was buried in the wilderness during Israel's forty-year wandering in it—one year for every day the faithless spies spent spying out the land of Canaan:—

And your children shall be shepherds in the wilderness for forty years, and shall suffer for your faithlessness, until the last of your dead bodies lies in the wilderness. According to the number of the days in which you spied out the land, forty days, for every day a year, you shall bear your iniquity, forty years, and you shall know my displeasure." I the LORD *have spoken; surely I will do thus to all this wicked congregation gathered together against me: in this wilderness they shall come to a full end, and there they shall die* (Numbers 14:33–35).

The LORD'S *anger was kindled on that day and he swore, saying, "Surely none of the people who came up out of Egypt,* **from twenty years old and upward**, *shall see the land that I swore to give to Abraham, to Isaac, and to Jacob, because they have not unreservedly followed me— none except Caleb son* *of Jephunneh the Kenizzite and Joshua son of Nun, for they have unreservedly followed the L*ORD*." And the L*ORD*'s anger was kindled against Israel, and he made them wander in the wilderness for forty years, until all the generation that had done evil in the sight of the L*ORD *had disappeared* (Numbers 32:10–13).

Assuming that over the forty years Israel continued to reproduce like the faithless generation that fell in the wilderness, we could reasonably expect to have an approximate Israelite population of somewhere around one million, eight hundred ten thousand, six hundred fifty (1,810,650) that entered upon the conquest of the Promised Land under the leadership of General Joshua.

Sin and unrighteousness = Wars
Wars = loss of life and loss of land

From its inception as a nation, Israel has been involved in fighting wars, often against itself, spilling the blood of its own people. Most of the wars came about due to sin committed by both kings and their subjects. King David, who was a man after God's own heart, raised Israel to its pinnacle of greatness. After

David, his son Solomon ruled, but Solomon's heart was turned away from the Lord by the many women he loved: —

King Solomon, however, loved many foreign women besides Pharaoh's daughter—Moabites, Ammonites, Edomites, Sidonians and Hittites
(1Kings 11:1).

*Among his wives were seven hundred princesses and three hundred concubines; and **his wives turned away his heart*** (1Kings 11:3).

Solomon did not cleave to the LORD all the days of his life like his father David had done. Solomon did much evil in the sight of the LORD: —

Solomon did evil in the sight of the LORD, and did not fully follow the LORD, as did his father David. Then Solomon built a high place for Chemosh the abomination of Moab, on the hill that is east of Jerusalem, and for Molech the abomination of the people of Ammon. And he did likewise for all his foreign wives, who burned incense and sacrificed to their gods (1Kings 11:6).

Following the death of King Solomon, his son Rehoboam took the throne, but due to Solomon's sins the LORD GOD quickly had Rehoboam's inherited kingdom stripped of the ten northern tribes. Those ten tribes, which were cut off in a revolt against Rehoboam's rule, formed Israel's northern kingdom, the kingdom of Israel, which established its capital in Samaria. The northern kingdom, the kingdom of Israel, was led by Jeroboam who, to prevent the people from going to Jerusalem to worship the Lord, made two golden calves for his subjects to worship, placing one in Bethel and the other in Dan (1Kings 12:30).

Rehoboam was left ruling over only two tribes, Judah and Benjamin, which became the southern kingdom of Judah. There was perpetual war between the two kingdoms and they sometimes allied themselves with outside powers against each other. It was virtually a very long, drawn out civil war in which Judah, with Jerusalem remaining as its capital, unsuccessfully fought to bring the ten northern tribes back under its sovereignty. The two kingdoms remained separate states until both were captured at different times by armies from the north.

In 721 BCE. Assyria swept out of the north, captured the northern kingdom and took the people of the ten tribes into captivity. From there they became lost to history and are today known historically as the ten lost tribes. However, during preceding years, thousands from the tribes in the northern kingdom of Israel who refused to worship Jeroboam's golden calves left their ancestral homes and joined themselves to the southern kingdom of Judah in order to continue temple worship of the LORD. Therefore, in reality, there never was a loss of ten tribes, the righteous ones from among those tribes had joined the southern kingdom of Judah. The northern kingdom of Israel was majorly idolatrous and its many kings were extremely corrupt, thus Israel sowed the wind and reaped the whirlwind.

The southern kingdom of Judah lasted around one hundred and thirty-four years longer than the northern kingdom of Israel. This was largely due to most of its kings being less corrupted by idolatry, but it was still way too sinful to escape God's wrath and the punitive punishment He decreed for it. A seventy-year exile from the land was decreed and, following the mandated exile, forty-two thousand three hundred sixty Israelites from the southern kingdom and those from the kingdom of Israel who had joined themselves to Judah, returned to the Land (Ezra 2:64), along with some servants and livestock.

So few returning to the land was in accordance with the word of the LORD brought by the prophet Jeremiah:—

The LORD showed me two baskets of figs placed before the temple of the LORD. This was after King Nebuchadrezzar of Babylon had taken into exile from Jerusalem King Jeconiah son of Jehoiakim of Judah, together with the officials of Judah, the artisans, and the smiths, and had brought them to Babylon. One basket had very good figs, like first-ripe figs, but the other basket had very bad figs, so bad that they could not be eaten. And the LORD said to me, "What do you see, Jeremiah?" I said, "Figs, the good figs very good, and the bad figs very bad, so bad that they cannot be eaten."

Then the word of the LORD came to me: Thus says the LORD, the God of

Israel: Like these good figs, so I will regard as good the exiles from Judah, whom I have sent away from this place to the land of the Chaldeans. I will set my eyes upon them for good, and I will bring them back to this land

(Jeremiah 24:1–6).

But thus says the LORD: Like the bad figs that are so bad they cannot be eaten, so will I treat King Zedekiah of Judah, his officials, the remnant of Jerusalem who remain in this land, and those who live in the land of Egypt. I will make them a horror, an evil thing, to all the kingdoms of the earth—a disgrace, a byword, a taunt, and a curse in all the places where I shall drive them. And I will send sword, famine, and pestilence upon them, until they are utterly destroyed from the land that I gave to them and their ancestors

(Jeremiah 24:8–10).

Those forty-two thousand three hundred sixty Israelites who returned were the good figs, together with the righteous ones that joined Judah from the kingdom of Israel, those who refused to worship the golden calves that Jeroboam had set up in the northern kingdom.

As stated earlier (according to an historian), over the centuries the Israelites have only had full possession of all their land for little more than a cumulative two hundred years; their sin always brought an end to full or partial occupation one way or another.

It has been continued sin that has brought disasters and horrendous loss of life upon Israel, like the loss of the generation in the wilderness when the Israelites came up out of Egypt. Israel has been steeped in sin since its inception and has had to pay a terrible human price. Israel's continual sinning against its Creator is by far the major reason for the huge discrepancy between the populations of China, India, and Israel. The LORD, through Moses, gave warning of what would befall the Israelites if they continued on their path of sin. It would not just be disasters and loss of life, but also loss of length of days in the land: —

> *I call heaven and earth to witness against*
> *you today that I have set before you life*
> *and death, blessings and curses. Choose*
> *life so that you and your descendants*
> *may live, loving the LORD your God,*
> *obeying him, and holding fast to him;*

for that means life to you and length of days, so that you may live in the land that the LORD swore to give to your ancestors, to Abraham, to Isaac, and to Jacob (Deuteronomy 30:19–20).

Pogroms—massacres of Jews—in days of yore throughout Europe and Russia for hundreds of years was capped in the early to mid-1940s by Germany's Adolf Hitler and his Nazi regime. Hitler and his cadres worked to devise a means to massacre European Jews on a scale of murder never before seen by mankind. Hitler's "Final Solution" for the eradication of Jews in Europe began with roundups and mass shootings of hundreds of Jews by German troops whenever they captured towns and villages containing Jews. As German troops captured large cities, shooting thousands of Jews and burying them in mass graves, was soon considered to be both unnecessarily expensive and time consuming. For Hitler, his systematic murder of Jews needed to be industrialized and so death camps were created for this purpose.

The death camps built by the Nazis throughout Eastern Europe were literally extermination camps, nothing less than slaughterhouses for processing Jews. These camps predominantly used a cyanide-based gas called Zyclon-B, which was administered via overhead showers after scores of Jews had been herded naked into the 'shower rooms.' After gold teeth were extracted from the corpses they were burnt in crematorium ovens built specifically for that purpose. At war's end in 1945 some six million Jews had been murdered by the Germans. Today, the world remembers the Nazi genocide of the European Jews as "The Holocaust." In addition, several million homosexuals, Roma Gypsies and mentally retarded persons were also exterminated by the Nazis.

A call for converts

Assimilation and intermarriage—most especially in western nations—has further depleted the remaining millions in the Jewish fold. Some Jewish organizations believe that without further adherents (converts) to Judaism the religion will eventually die out. According to an October 2020 demographic study by the London-based Institute for Jewish Policy Research, the Jewish share of the population of Europe is as low now as it was a thousand years ago and is declining even further, which is a harbinger of the dire straits the Jewish religion faces in Europe. America and elsewhere in the West face similar declining figures for Jewish populations.

Arnold Eisen, chancellor of the Jewish Theological Seminary, wrote a *Wall Street Journal* Op-Ed for July 24, 2014 titled "Wanted: Converts to Judaism." In the article, Eisen wrote:—

> I am asking the rabbis of the Conservative movement to use every means to explicitly and strongly advocate for conversion, bringing potential converts close and actively making the case for them to commit to Judaism. I am asking Jewish leaders to provide the funding needed for programs, courses and initiatives that will place conversion at the center of Jewish consciousness and the community's agenda.

Some organizations today are immersing themselves into funding outreach programs to Gentiles with the goal of converting non-Jews and bringing them into the fold. They obviously believe that if Jews do not spread their religion now, Judaism will not survive.

Whatever the reasons, Jews have been uncomfortable with proselytizing, but they have pursued it for millennia nevertheless and Yeshua (Jesus) did not mince words when he castigated the religious leaders of his day:

> *Woe to you, scribes and Pharisees, hypocrites! For you cross sea and land to make a single convert, and you make the new convert twice as much a child of hell as yourselves* (Matthew 23:15).

A Gentile who has converted to Judaism, is bound to all the doctrines and precepts of the Jewish religion, and is (supposedly) considered a full member of the Jewish people. The proselyte is circumcised as an adult and is immersed in a Jewish ritual bath (*mikvah*) to formally conclude the conversion process.

The written Word says that *"God created man in His own image"* (Genesis 1:7), but in reality, rabbis take Gentiles and *re-create them* into their own images, and this would no doubt have spawned Yeshua's (Jesus') rebuke concerning converts.

As already mentioned, converts to Judaism are 'supposedly' considered a full member of the Jewish people, but the actions of some Jewish religious leaders show that such a statement is somewhat absurd. Some years ago there was a hullabaloo in Israel when Jewish religious authorities were discussing printing "Convert" in Israeli Passports and on Israeli Identity Cards of those who had converted to Judaism. This showed that the religious authorities in Israel (Haredi) do not see converts as anything near being full members of the Jewish community and wanted to enshrine their religious bigotry and prejudice into law, forever setting converts in a category other than "Jew." Fortunately, reason prevailed after the public backlash and the idea was finally dropped. However, for those who do convert, and some actually appear and act more Jewish than Moses, say that when a matter is being discussed, those born Jews will dismiss the convert's opinion with, "You're only a convert, what do you know?"

There will never be full acceptance into the Jewish fold for converts, no matter how far they may immerse themselves into the Jewish way of life: sporting long earlocks and wearing the preferred, but ridiculous black seventeenth-century nobleman's clothing with trouser cuffs tucked into the socks. As an example of non-acceptance this writer can relate an exchange that took place in his presence in the early 1990s.

At that time this writer had a small factory manufacturing custom furniture and restoring antique furniture and, among other workers, this writer employed a young man in his mid-twenties for a period of some months. When this writer took David on as an untrained helper this writer knew he would not be staying permanently, because, his heart was really wanting to work in magazine publishing and working for this writer was merely a means to that end. The day came when David excitedly showed this writer a small-circulation magazine published locally that was seeking a manager. David wanted to know if this writer would let him go if he applied for the position and got it. This writer knew it was where his heart lay and encouraged him to apply.

About two weeks later David told this writer that he had been accepted for the position and that he would be leaving at the end of the month. This writer was sorry to lose him, because he was a good worker and was also very trustworthy.

This writer began advertising for a replacement for David, specifically targeting craftsmen in furniture restoration. One man, Gary, a black coated ultra-Orthodox Jew showed this writer his work portfolio, which was impressive; he was an American-born immigrant from New York. Gary was meticulous in his work and with Judaism. He told this writer that he had converted to Judaism some years earlier and that in Judaism he had found his niche.

After Gary began working for this writer, young David came to visit, proudly showing a hot-off-the-press copy of his magazine, which he had set up and produced entirely on his own. But within seconds of entering the factory David saw Gary with his *payot* (sidelocks), busily working in a white shirt and black trousers tucked into his socks. David looked at Gary, then looked at this writer, and said to this writer, "What's that converted *goy* doing here?" — *goy* is a Jewish name for a non-Jew. This writer was a bit taken aback, because Gary appeared to be the very essence of an ultra-Orthodox Jew.

This writer knew Gary was a convert to Judaism, because he had told him so, but young David, being born Jewish, instinctively knew Gary was a convert. Gary had proudly told this writer that he had found his niche, his fulfillment, in Judaism, but a natural-born Jew, in the briefest of seconds, recognized Gary as a convert. Gary would have been mortified had he known what David said about him being a converted *goy*. This writer then understood what most converts to Judaism must go through, never being part of the Jewish people, just being a converted *goy* helping to prop up a dying religion.

Jews are now trying rather desperately to gain converts to Judaism from among the Gentiles (whom they virtually despise), because the Jews, as an ethnic group, are a dying race. Abraham, whose name was formerly Abram until the Lord changed it (Genesis 17:5), was descended from Eber, making Abraham an Eberite, and from Eberite we get *ivrit*, which is the word for Hebrew—thus *"Abraham the Hebrew"* (Genesis 14:13.).

Abraham's descendants were Jews, a national race of people, but in our day this race of Jew has been flipped into a religion that is practiced. All true Jews have a distinct DNA, which no number of conversion classes, circumcision rituals, or immersion in a kosher *mikvah* can make a convert a Jew. Israel's religious leaders will sometimes run DNA tests to establish a prospective immigrant's Jewishness and eligibility for citizenship.

Thus, with modern Judaism leaning toward conversions, the Jew "race" will eventually be reduced to a token few; the mass will be converts who will never be Jews, only converted *goyim*. It is interesting to note that if a Jew is secular and does not practice Judaism, he is still regarded as a Jew. But if a Christian becomes worldly and does not practice the teachings of Yeshua (Jesus), that person is no longer Christian.

Israel's first prime minister, David Ben-Gurion, annually allowed four hundred Haredi Jews to have militarily service deferment. Once the Likud party got into power it made ultra-Orthodox political parties its allies in the Knesset, and to ensure they remained loyal to Likud they have allowed annual deferments for more than ten thousand Haredim. Their yeshivas (Jewish seminaries) have long since become budgeted and a single student can cost the state more than NIS 4,000 (USD 1,180) per month; property taxes and healthcare costs for married students have been reduced well below normal rates.

Haredim generally have large families and there is a strong relationship between religiosity and fertility; birth records show that the fertility rate of ultra-Orthodox women is three times that of secular Jewish women. Israeli government data show ultra-Orthodox Haredi women give birth to forty babies per thousand women, while women of the general population give birth to twenty-one babies per thousand.

Some Israeli ultra-Orthodox families live entirely on the child allowance alone. Only a small percentage of Haredim, who make up eight percent of the working age population, are employed as they shun work almost as vociferously as they do military conscription. Ultra-Orthodox Haredim comprise around eleven percent of Israel's population and by and large they only ever take from the state, never giving to it.

The average Israeli has a negative view of the ultra-Orthodox because they themselves work, pay taxes and complete years of military service to defend their country.

It is projected that Ultra-Orthodox Haredim will comprise thirty-five percent of the population by the year 2059, which, without serious changes, will be unsustainable for the nation.

Many thousands of ultra-Orthodox have shown themselves to be totally lawless. Beginning in early 2020 Israel was hit by the Covid-19 virus pandemic and due to flouting of Health Ministry regulations Israel soon had the highest number of infections per capita in the world — in fact three times higher than the next heavily infected country.

The government mandated lockdowns in all cities where the virus was spreading out of control. Large gatherings were forbidden, including weddings and yeshiva prayer gatherings. However, by the third week of lockdowns forty percent of new infections were in the Haredi population, because they ignored face masks, social distancing, and large gatherings. The general population became angry with the Haredim because they put the general population at risk. Deaths shot up beyond two thousand nine hundred persons and fifty-five percent of the deaths of those over sixty-five years of age were ultra-Orthodox.

Antisemitism

The scourge of antisemitism and antisemitic attacks on Jews, Jewish cemeteries and Jewish property has been steadily rising since the start of this current millennium. The bulk of these attacks is due to the freedom of emigration for Muslims into Western countries. Jews and Israel are both anathema to the great majority of Muslims. Muslims suckle hatred of Jews and Israel with their mothers' milk. The Muslim holy book, the Qur'an, is replete with hatred of Jews and Israel and calls for the destruction of Israel and death for the Jews. Muslims feed on this written hatred every day and their Imams delight in spewing antisemitic hatred from the pulpits of mosques.

Another reason for antisemitism is the very noticeable clothing fashions that thousands upon thousands of ultra-religious Jews habitually wear. Wearing seventeenth-century nobleman's clothes (plus fur *shtreimel* hats for married men) distinguishes ultra-Orthodox Jews from 'normal' people and makes them into a laughing stock, which brings derision, prejudice and hatred. For most ultra-Orthodox Jews the ridiculous attire is traditional, but tradition can be stronger than tempered steel to break.

As one Haredi rabbi explained, the special dress means that "I can't stand in line for an inappropriate movie. I can't get angry at someone cutting me in line" — at least not without dragging the whole ancient edifice of Judaism with him into the fight.

Haredim are a very distinctive community, painted in a very identifiable palette. You can locate them easily in a synagogue, photograph them with their *shtreimels* and top hats. Made from the tails of sables and foxes, the *shtreimel* hats can cost as much as $5,000. The Haredim are almost the only widespread users of fur in Israel, which enjoys a warm Mediterranean climate.

The upshot of all this is that ultra-Orthodox Haredim are not unaware of how they appear to the outside world; that awareness is central to their culture.

The Chabad (also known as Lubavitch) ultra-Orthodox Haredi movement numbering

hundreds of thousands, do not draw ire
from the populace like the ultra-Orthodox
dressed in seventeenth-century noblemen's
attire. Chabad is one of the world's largest
and best known Haredi movements with
outreach activities in many countries; the
men wear black suits and trilby hats and do
not draw adverse attention like other Haredi
movements unless they dominate an entire
neighborhood area, turning it into a virtual
ghetto.

One new man

Until God's New Covenant was preached
by Yeshua (Jesus) only Jews and a handful
of Gentile proselytes had a real awareness of
God Almighty. However, from the beginning
of time it was formulated in the mind of the
LORD to first offer forgiveness of sins and
eternal life *to the Jews first*, then reach out
and gather in all the Gentile nations as well,
to make one flock of righteous people. This
was repeatedly made known through His
prophets; for example:—

> *Praise the LORD, all you Gentiles!*
> *Laud Him, all you peoples!*
> (Psalms 117:1)

And in that day there shall be a Root of Jesse,

Who shall stand as a banner to the people;

For the Gentiles shall seek Him,

And His resting place shall be glorious
(Isaiah 11:10).

The Gentiles shall come to Your light,

And kings to the brightness of Your rising (Isaiah 60:3).

And this plan became operative through the New Covenant, following the sacrificial death of Yeshua (Jesus) on the cross: —

For he himself is our peace, who has made the two groups one and has destroyed the barrier, the dividing wall of hostility, by setting aside in his flesh the law with its commands and regulations. His purpose was to create in himself one new man out of the two, thus making peace, and in one body to reconcile both of them to God through the cross, by which he put to death their hostility (Ephesians 2:14–18).

However, peace between Jews and Gentiles never happened on a grand scale. Many Jews, predominantly rabbis, have fought, often violently, against the teachings of Yeshua (Jesus) and against those who have received salvation through him. As Yeshua. (Jesus) said: —

Woe to you, teachers of the law and Pharisees, hypocrites! For you shut the kingdom of heaven in people's faces. You neither enter yourselves nor allow those who would enter to go in

(Matthew 23:13).

In teachings to his disciples Yeshua (Jesus) foretold the divisions and battles within families that would come because of him:

Do you think that I have come to bring peace to the earth? No, I tell you, but rather division! From now on five in one household will be divided, three against two and two against three; they will be divided: father against son and son against father, mother against daughter and daughter against mother, mother-in-law against her daughter-in-law and daughter-in-law against mother-in-law

(Luke 12:51–53).

Is that not the truth? In Jewish families, many parents will disown their children if they believe Yeshua (Jesus) to be the Messiah. Some will go so far as holding burial services for sons or daughters. Some will never speak the name of a child believing in Yeshua (Jesus) again. Many adults have lost their employment because they believe Yeshua (Jesus) to be the Messiah. Numbers have been turned out of their rental apartments by landlords for the same reason.

The hatred of Yeshua (Jesus) by Jews is primarily because many anti-Jew purges and massacres were carried out by those falsely claiming to be followers of Yeshua (Jesus), and the violence and murder is perpetrated because the perpetrators believe, falsely, that Jews alone killed Yeshua (Jesus). The Jews did not physically crucify Yeshua (Jesus), but they did initiate the crucifixion and called for his death on a cross. Following a mock trial before the High Priest the chief priests and religious leaders took Yeshua (Jesus) to the Roman Governor Pontius Pilate, because they wanted Yeshua (Jesus) dead but did not have the power to carry out his death sentence. Even Pilate understood that the religious leaders were acting out of envy and he wanted to let Yeshua (Jesus) go, but the chief priests stirred up the crowds and had them shout "Crucify him, crucify him!" until an uproar ensued that was quickly getting out of control. Finally: —

> *Pilate ... took some water and washed his hands before the crowd, saying, "I am innocent of this man's blood; see to it yourselves." Then the people as a whole answered, "His blood be on us and on our children!"* (Matthew 27:24–25).

This is not antisemitism, this is history written down by a Jew named Matthew for other Jews to read.

Pontius Pilate was the Roman Governor of the region, as such he had all the power of Rome behind him. When he washed his hands before the crowd calling for the crucifixion of Yeshua (Jesus) he was effectively declaring both himself and Rome free from any subsequent fallout. When Pilate said to the crowd, "*See to it yourselves,*" he passed the matter back to the Jews, who responded with, "*His blood be on us and on our children!*" and it has been.

The New Covenant is in the blood of Yeshua (Jesus), and what has befallen the Jews since the day of the foolish declaration (above) shows the accuracy of the Scripture:—

Death and life are in the power of the tongue, and those who love it will eat its fruit (Proverbs 18:21).

This was just another reason for the great discrepancy between the Chinese, Indian and Israeli populations.

In handing over an innocent man for crucifixion, a man whom Pilate knew to be guiltless of the charges the chief priests and rulers had vocalized against Yeshua (Jesus), Pilate abused his position as Governor rather than administer justice before a rowdy, hate-filled mob. The Jews called down a curse upon themselves, which remains in effect until the day they say of Yeshua (Jesus): *"Blessed is he who comes in the name of the Lord"* (Matthew 23:39).

It is pointless for Jews to continue trying to evade their involvement in the crucifixion of Yeshua (Jesus), because it is well documented in historical records as being genuine; such records having been placed under the microscopes of the worlds of academia and history. Admitting to their role in the process of crucifying Yeshua (Jesus) will help clear the air concerning it.

A stiff-necked Jewish nation that refuses to hear and believe God Almighty's words concerning His Messiah, together with a largely unbelieving, idolatrous Catholic Church, which primarily worships the Virgin Mary instead of Yeshua (Jesus) is a sure recipe for continued conflict. Even some Protestant denominations hold anti-Jew or anti-Israel positions, but the great majority of evangelical Christians are very supportive of the Jews and the Jewish state. The Jews have a legitimate grievance against non-Jews and non-Jews have a legitimate grievance against the Jews. Only the recognition and acceptance of Yeshua (Jesus) by Jew and non-Jew alike will end the millennia-long bitterness: —

For he himself is our peace, who has made the two groups one and has destroyed the barrier, the dividing wall of hostility, by setting aside in his flesh the law with its commands and regulations. His purpose was to create in himself one new man out of the two, thus making peace, and in one body to reconcile both of them to God through the cross, by which he put to death their hostility (Ephesians 2:14–18).

However, when we look at the history of Israel and the actions of many of its kings and leaders during past millennia, we see that it was the result of unfettered sin that brought the great and terrible destructions upon the Jewish people. God Almighty frequently used non-Jews as His instruments of punitive punishment. With there only being two types of peoples, Jews and non-Jews, the choices for the LORD were limited.

God Almighty says *"Israel is my firstborn son"* (Exodus 4:22) therefore, as God's firstborn, Israel receives a *"double portion"* (Deuteronomy 21:17), not only in wealth and intelligence, but also in punishment for her sin. Without doubt the Jews are highly intelligent. Comprising only 1.13 percent of the world's population (2020) Jews from 1901 – 90 were awarded 22 percent of all Nobel Prizes, but the intelligence of Jews seems to be limited to the sciences and finance, because in some areas, like remaining true to the LORD, and believing Yeshua (Jesus) is the nation's promised Messiah, they also show themselves to be unintelligent, stubborn and somewhat obtuse.

As mentioned earlier, there was a total of 14.7 million Jews worldwide at the end of 2018. Adding the six million murdered in the Holocaust still only brings us to a total of 20.7 million, plus we could add a hypothetical progeny of perhaps 50 million that was lost to those who died in the Holocaust, which would give us a hypothetical total to 70.7 million.

The population of China in 2018 was 1.393 billion and the population of India in 2018 was 1.353 billion. The Holocaust was the worst genocide ever committed in world history, yet even our hypothetical 70.7 million Jewish population it is impossible to explain the huge difference between the populations of Israel, China and India, which all have similar lengths of history and fertilities. Even if we double, triple or quadruple the hypothetical progeny number we still cannot get Israel's current population within reach of China or India. Only God Almighty's handing out of punitive punishments for sin can explain Israel's shortfall of a billion-plus in population. It is past time Jews stopped blaming Gentiles for the tragedies that have befallen them and begin to sincerely repent of their sin and hypocritical self-perceived whiteness of character. Claiming to be "righteous inside and out" does not stand up against the facts. As the Good Book divinely says: —

> *The wages of the righteous is life, but the earnings of the wicked are sin and death* (Proverbs 10:16)

> *For the wages of sin is death, but the gift of God is eternal life in Christ Jesus our Lord* (Romans 6:23).

to the Jew first

With God Almighty it has always been a case of *"to the Jew first."* The Jews were the first to receive God's law and commandments, the first Covenant, written with God's finger on tablets of stone, the covenant which they broke before it even arrived in the camp. Only the pleading of Moses on their behalf prevented God Almighty from wiping all the tribes of Israel out even at that early stage (Exodus 32:10). Another set of tablets were prepared and God Almighty wrote His law and commandments again, but He has been forced to say of His people:—

> *They have all fallen away, they are all alike perverse; there is no one who does good, no, not one* (Psalms 53:3).

At the time of His choosing, God Almighty began the phasing out of plan A, the Sinaitic covenant, and putting His plan B into action. His only begotten Son, Yeshua (Jesus), was born in Bethlehem and then some thirty-three years later gave his life and shed his blood on the cross at Calvary. His sacrificial death was an atonement, it was made in order to wash away the sins of the Jewish people, but they were and still are having none of it. The Jews flogged, imprisoned and killed those who shared the message of the forgiveness of sins and everlasting life for all who would obey and receive Yeshua (Jesus) as Israel's Messiah. God Almighty had long ago purposed that His love and salvation was to be first offered to the Jews and Yeshua (Jesus) was committed to his Father's plan and instructed his twelve principal disciples accordingly:—

> *Jesus [Yeshua] sent out these twelve,*
> *instructing them, "Go nowhere among*

*the Gentiles and enter no town of the
Samaritans, but go rather to the lost
sheep of the house of Israel"*

(Matthew 10:5).

God Almighty appointed and ordained Saul
of Tarsus (also known as Paul) as the Apostle
to the Gentiles. Before God's call Saul was a
Pharisee, a member to the strictest Jewish sect
and he persecuted the early Jewish Christians.
Saul forced the new Christians to blaspheme,
bound and imprisoned them, and when they
were put to death he cast his vote against them.
Saul was on his way to Damascus in Syria with
letters from the High Priest and the Council
of Elders to bind Jewish Christians and bring
them back to Jerusalem for punishment. As
he neared Damascus Yeshua (Jesus) revealed
himself to Saul in a light brighter than the
midday sun, which shone all around him.
When he opened his eyes Saul was unable
to see because something like scales covered
his eyes and he required someone to lead
him by the hand. After being prayed for in
Damascus by a local follower of Yeshua
(Jesus) and filled with God Almighty's Spirit,
the scales fell from his eyes and he set out to
preach the gospel of the New Covenant. Saul

faced death numerous times and was often imprisoned for preaching repentance toward God and remission of sins through faith in Yeshua (Jesus). His God-given task was not an easy one to fulfill in a hostile world and he recorded some of his troubles:—

Five times from the Jews I received forty lashes minus one. Three times I was beaten with rods; once I was stoned; three times I was shipwrecked; a night and a day I have been in the deep; constantly on the move, in dangers of waters, in dangers from robbers, in dangers from my own countrymen, in dangers from the Gentiles, in dangers in the city, in dangers in the wilderness, in dangers in the sea, in dangers from false brethren (2Corinthians 11:24–24).

Yet with all his troubles, with all his beatings and being imprisoned in chains for years, Saul, the Jew born anew, could say:—

*I am not ashamed of the gospel of Messiah, for it is the power of God to salvation for everyone who believes, for the **Jew first** and also for the Greek [non-Jew]* (Romans 1:16).

Initially, Saul and his traveling companions preached to their own countrymen, to the Jews first, in their synagogues and meeting places in the diaspora: —

To you first, God, having raised up His Servant Jesus, sent him to bless you, in turning away every one of you from your iniquities (Acts 3:26).

Some would pay heed to the divine offer of remission of sins and receipt of eternal life, but many of those who did not embrace Yeshua (Jesus) would rail against Saul and his companions, cause public disturbances and endeavor to turn those who believed away from their new-found faith.

Finding much more openness among the non-Jews and being on the receiving end of so much vitriol and violence from the Jews, Saul, (also known as Paul), decided to concentrate upon and primarily direct his preaching to non-Jews, thereby fulfilling his God-given call as the Apostle to the Gentiles: —

Then both Paul and Barnabas spoke out boldly, saying, "It was necessary that the word of God should be spoken first to you. Since you reject it and judge

> *yourselves to be unworthy of eternal*
> *life, we are now turning to the Gentiles*
> (Acts 13:46).

The Roman conquest of Israel forced many thousands of Israelites to flee the land and there were Jews in almost every city in Asia. Saul shared the gospel of God's remission of sins and eternal life to all who believed Yeshua (Jesus) was God Almighty's Son and Israel's Messiah and King. Saul's message of salvation was directed at all his listeners, but it was still *to the Jew first*: —

> *There will be tribulation and anguish,*
> *on every soul of man who does evil,*
> *of the **Jew first** and also of the Greek*
> *[non-Jew]; but glory, honor, and peace*
> *to everyone who works what is good, to*
> *the **Jew first** and also to the Greek [non-*
> *Jew]* (Romans 2:9–10).

The Scriptures tell us repeatedly that not one person ever kept the written law. To break the least commandment meant the whole law was broken. The advent of Yeshua (Jesus) put an end to the bondage to the written law. The New Covenant brings freedom from the law: —

Now we are discharged from the law, dead to that which held us captive, so that we are slaves not under the old written code but in the new life of the Spirit. (Romans 7:6).

God Almighty's Spirit brings abundant life for all who believe and embrace Yeshua (Jesus) in their heart when they are reborn from above. Eons ago, looking toward this momentous day for every individual, God promised to pour out His Spirit on all flesh: —

And it shall come to pass afterward, that I will pour out my Spirit on all flesh; your sons and your daughters shall prophesy, your old men shall dream dreams, and your young men shall see visions. Even on the male and female servants in those days I will pour out my Spirit

(Joel 2:28–29).

"Come now," says the Almighty, the High and Lofty One, "it is time for you to open your hearts and get into the outpouring of My Holy Spirit and the Spirit of My Son Yeshua (Jesus)." Are you, dear reader, whether you are Jew or Gentile, willing to have your entire being filled with God? The choice is yours to make.

Other Ramon Bennett titles by *Shekinah*

When Day and Night Cease: A prophetic study of world events and how prophecy concerning Israel affects the nations, the Church and you

SAGA: Israel and the demise of nations

Philistine: The Great Deception

The Wall: Prophecy, Politics and Middle East "Peace"

The Wilderness: Israel's Ultimate Wandering

GAZA: The Fallout From Premeditated Barbarianism

All My Tears (Ramon Bennett's auto biography)

Gospel (the four gospels blended into a single narrative)

No Other Name (the four blended gospels with some commentaries)

Abe (the life and example of Abraham, the father of faith)

My Cup Runneth Over (An ornate, cracked and chipped cup that was supernaturally made new again)

Apples Of Gold (Bible teaching on seventeen subjects)

The Green Olive Tree: *All The Promises of God In Him Are Yes and In Him Amen*

HiStory: The Birth, Life, And Death of Jesus Christ, Son of God, Redeemer of Mankind